DOLPHINS

What They Can Teach Us

DOLPHINS
What They Can Teach Us

Text by
Mary M. Cerullo

Photographs by
Jeffrey L. Rotman

DUTTON CHILDREN'S BOOKS
New York

For David Friedman, whose friendship and knowledge
of both the sea and life have meant so much—JLR

For Nan Hauser, who introduced me to her friends—MMC

ACKNOWLEDGMENTS

Thank you to Nan Hauser, Director of the New England Dolphin Outreach, Brunswick, Maine, and to Dana Carnegie, Director of Media Relations at the Dolphin Research Center, Grassy Key, Florida, for reviewing the manuscript. Their familiarity with current research and issues enriched these pages. Any errors are the author's, not theirs.—MMC

Thanks to the entire staff of Dolphin Reef in Eilat, Israel, and to Abdallah, the Bedouin of Nuweiba, Egypt. Without their help, the photographs in this book would not have been possible.—JLR

Photograph on page 38 copyright © Doug Perrine/Jeff Rotman Photography

Library of Congress Cataloging-in-Publication Data
Cerullo, Mary M.
Dolphins: what they can teach us / text by Mary M. Cerullo;
photographs by Jeffrey L. Rotman.
p.   cm.
Includes bibliographical references (p.   ) and index.
Summary: Focuses on the behavior of these large sea animals,
their interactions with humans, and ways in which dolphins
and people can benefit each other.
ISBN 0-525-65263-9
1. Dolphins—Juvenile literature. 2. Human-animal relationships—
Juvenile literature.   [1. Dolphins.   2. Human-animal relationships.]
I. Rotman, Jeffrey L., ill. II. Title.
QL737.C432C47   1999   599.53—DC21   97-34424   CIP   AC

Published in the United States by Dutton Children's Books,
a member of Penguin Putnam Inc.,
375 Hudson Street, New York, New York 10014

Designed by Charlotte Staub
Printed in Hong Kong
First Edition   10 9 8 7 6 5 4 3 2 1

Contents

Dolphins seem to enjoy being in the company of humans.

Chapter 1

A Little Knowledge

There once was a storybook character named Dr. Dolittle who marveled how wonderful it would be "If I could walk with the animals, talk to the animals, and they could talk with me." I wondered that myself when I went to the Florida Keys to spend a week with thirteen bottlenose dolphins at the Dolphin Research Center on Grassy Key. Some had been "retired" from animal parks, some from Navy research projects, and several had been born here. Carved from the mangroves and coral reef, the dolphins' pens were separated from the ocean by only a low fence to keep out sharks, debris, and curious humans.

I was dangling my legs from a dock overlooking the largest dolphin pool, an enclosure shared by three female dolphins and their offspring. I placed my hand flat on the surface of the murky green water. Within seconds a dolphin's fin tickled my palm. Tursi, a female dolphin, poked her head above the water. She turned on her side and studied me with one eye.

She zoomed off and returned a moment later with her son, Talon. He was three years old, quite old enough to be on his own. But his mom had already lost two calves, so she guarded this one closely. Ever ready for fun, he dove beneath the dock and surfaced with a slimy present of green seaweed. He tossed it playfully into my lap. I threw it back, and we played catch until his watchful mother hustled him back to her side.

I held my disposable underwater camera just below the surface and started clicking pictures. Almost immediately, I heard several dolphins echolocating on this curious object. At the same time, they began whistling, perhaps calling to their friends to come investigate. When I developed my photographs I had twenty fuzzy close-ups of passing fins, "smiling" faces, and peering eyes.

In a neighboring pool, Delphi and Kibby called out for attention with a chorus of whistles, chirps, and squawks. Unlike humans, dolphins have no vocal cords, so they don't need to open their mouths to "speak." But these two large males had watched how humans move their mouths when they made noises, so Kibby and Delphi politely did the same. Their jaws curved upward in permanent grins, and the wrinkles around their eyes looked like laugh lines.

Who could not be enchanted by such amiable creatures? I learned that they deserved their reputation for friendliness, playfulness, com-

A playful dolphin greets a visitor.

plex social behavior, and group loyalty. Their speed and agility prove they are ideally designed for ocean living.

Several years ago, some scientists theorized that dolphins have a spoken language all their own, which the researchers dubbed *dolphin-ese*. The size and complexity of their brains led various researchers to claim that dolphin intelligence matches (depending on the opinion of the particular researcher) humans, chimpanzees, dogs, or parrots.

Many of the scientists who study dolphins today feel that comparing dolphins to humans or to other animals does not give them credit for their own singular adaptations and abilities. They outswim, outdive, and even outplay humans. Dolphins produce sounds we cannot—sonar clicks, squeaks, and signature whistles—but scientists as yet have found no evidence of a dolphin "language." Instead of trying to describe dolphins in human terms, they feel we should focus on how they are unique and how they got that way.

The Dolphin Family Tree

Dolphins are small, toothed whales. They belong to the group known as cetaceans (from the Latin word *cetus*, meaning large sea animal), which includes all whales, dolphins, and porpoises. In the past, the terms *dolphin* and *porpoise* had often been used interchangeably, but a dolphin has a pointed snout and streamlined body, while a porpoise has a rounded snout and a slightly rounder build. Scientists distinguish between them by the shape of their teeth. Porpoises have spade-shaped teeth; dolphins have cone-shaped teeth.

Identifying the different kinds of dolphins can be confusing, partly because they are so widely distributed and because many species are found only in the open ocean, so they are hard to capture and classify. By various estimates, there are between thirty and forty species of dolphins, including some species we commonly call whales, such as killer whales (orcas) and pilot whales. Bottlenose dolphins (*Tursiops truncatus*) are one of the most wide-ranging species. They live along tropical and temperate coasts around the world. Other species of dolphins frequent frigid waters, like the Atlantic white-sided dolphin seen from the Gulf of St. Lawrence to the North Sea, and the hourglass dolphin that cruises Antarctic waters.

All life originated in the sea some three billion years ago. Animals only began to colonize the land after plants, insects, and other food sources settled there. It's hard to believe that an animal so well adapted to life in the sea could be related to animals that once roamed the land, but scientists believe that the ancestors of whales and dolphins were related to the ancestors of cows and horses.

For some reason, probably to find food, the descendants of these animals returned to the sea. It must have been a gradual move. These earliest dolphins and whales, like otters and seals of today, were probably still linked to the land. They may have hunted along the shoreline in marshy areas and then in shallow seas before evolving into full-time ocean dwellers. As new fossils of ancient ancestors are uncovered, scientists now suspect the forerunners of today's whales and dolphins may have moved onto and off the land several times.

Dolphins' ancestors first appeared about 11 million years ago. Humans appeared some 200,000 years ago. With a headstart of over 10 million years, it's no wonder dolphins have a lot to teach us!

What Characteristics Do We Share?

Dolphins and humans have a lot in common. We are both mammals. We nurse our young, which are born alive, not hatched from eggs. Mammals breathe air. A dolphin must come to the surface to breathe through a blowhole on the top of its head. When it dives, the blowhole closes. Instead of breathing continuously, as we do, a dolphin takes a breath and holds it until the next time it surfaces. (This way, it doesn't try to take a breath underwater by mistake.) Unlike us, dolphins have to "think" to breathe rather than "think" to hold their breath.

Both dolphins and humans are warm-blooded. A dolphin's internal body temperature is just a fraction lower than a human's 98.6° Fahrenheit. Because water removes body heat 25 times faster than air, dolphins must be more efficient at conserving heat than we landlubbers.

Two dolphins lift their heads out of the water to give their trainer a hug, clearly showing their blowholes.

Blubber is the key, that thick fatty layer just beneath the skin that insulates them from the chilling water. Blubber also streamlines their shape, acts as an energy reserve, and makes them buoyant. The arrangement of blood vessels in their fins and flippers also helps conserve body heat. Arteries carrying warm blood away from the heart are surrounded by blood vessels returning blood that has been cooled as it circulated through the body. In this way, some heat is exchanged between the blood vessels rather than being lost to the environment.

Mammals also have hair or fur, but you'd be hard pressed to find much hair on a dolphin. A newborn dolphin does have a few whiskers on its snout, which usually fall out by the time it is a week old. However, the openings that held the hair—the *follicle pits*—remain, so if you look closely at a dolphin's snout, you can see where it once had hair. Why might it be an advantage *not* to have hair? Some champion swimmers shave their heads and their legs to reduce the drag of water on their bodies and increase their speed. Could they be imitating dolphins?

Unanswered Questions

The United States Navy has been studying dolphins to learn about their hydrodynamics, echolocation, and deep-diving ability in order to apply these principles to the design of Navy ships and submarines. They have trained dolphins to locate and even retrieve tools and wreckage on the ocean floor. Other scientists are also interested in dolphins' adaptations to the sea, but, even more, they are interested in understanding how they behave and how their bodies work in order for humans to better care for sick and healthy dolphins in captivity and in the wild.

Some of the questions that most intrigue researchers today are:

How do dolphins communicate with each other?

How complex is dolphin society?

How do dolphins learn?

Can dolphins be taught a language invented by humans?

What can humans do to help dolphins worldwide?

Although people have been studying dolphins for thousands of years, we still have much to learn about them. There is a saying that "A little knowledge is a dangerous thing," but in the case of dolphins what little we already know about them just intrigues us to find out more. The next generation of marine biologists, dolphin trainers, and animal behaviorists have a lot to discover.

A dolphin's streamlined body helps it glide gracefully through the water.

Chapter 2

Survival
in the Sea

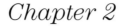

A half a dozen dolphins materialized from out of the blue ocean to ride the bow waves of a passing freighter. Despite the fact that the ship was speeding forward at 25 mph, the dolphins had no trouble keeping up with it. They dove, leaped, and looped around each other like Air Force jets at an aerial show. Dolphins have been called living submarines, but in fact, submarine designers would love to create machines as streamlined and as fluid as these creatures. After many minutes the dolphins disappeared as suddenly as they had come.

Adaptations to Ocean Living

You only have to watch a dolphin swim for a few seconds to see that it is perfectly proportioned to penetrate the waves. Its streamlined shape and smooth skin allow water to glide over it. A dolphin's skin feels like the skin on your wrist, but softer, because it is shed constantly to be replaced by even smoother skin. The smoother the skin the less the resistance it offers as the dolphin passes through the water.

A dolphin's tail beats up and down, not sideways like a fish's. A few quick strokes power it forward at great speed, drive it deep into the sea, or propel it to the surface to take a breath. Although dolphins usually surface to breathe two or three times a minute, ocean-going dolphins

The powerful tail of a dolphin beats up and down, not side to side as a fish's does.

regularly dive to 200 to 300 feet for five to eight minutes at a time. A dolphin can dive twice as deep as most human scuba divers can, and certainly faster.

The Navy is interested in learning how dolphins avoid a problem that plagues human divers who try to return to the surface too quickly—"the bends." When a human dives, the increasing pressure forces nitrogen from his air tank into his bloodstream. If he returns to the surface rapidly, the nitrogen changes into bubbles in the blood, which sometimes break, causing excruciating pain and even death.

When a dolphin dives past 230 feet (70 meters), its lungs and rib cage partially collapse. This keeps air from passing from the lungs into the rest of the body, so nitrogen cannot dissolve in its blood. At this depth, the pressure of the surrounding water is so great that the dolphin's body is compressed into a denser, smaller shape, which causes the animal to fall like a rock, according to Navy researcher Terrie Williams. Since the dolphin is no longer using energy to descend, she says, it doesn't burn up oxygen stored in its blood and in muscle cells.

Even the dolphin's color pattern is designed for survival in the sea. When viewed by a predator from above, its gray back blends in with the dark depths. A predator from below would find it hard to distinguish a dolphin's white belly from the sunlit surface of the sea.

How dolphins communicate is still something of a mystery. Unlike humans, they do not have vocal cords.

Chapter 3

How Dolphins Communicate

❧

Water conducts sound four and a half times faster than air does, so sound should be even more important to sea creatures than it is to land animals. Dolphins do indeed have excellent hearing, even though researcher Darlene Ketten has found that the earholes on the sides of their heads no longer open to the surface. They can also make a fascinating array of sounds. Dolphins produce two kinds of sounds: echolocation—a series of rapid clicks—and vocalizations—various noises they use to communicate. A dolphin can produce both kinds of sounds simultaneously because one comes from its blowhole and another from its forehead.

Echolocation

Imagine what it would be like to see with your ears. Echolocation, also called *sonar*, is the way dolphins locate and distinguish between objects underwater. The dolphin sends out a sound and listens for the echo. It allows the dolphin to navigate through dark or murky water without slamming into submarine mountains or hungry sharks.

Dolphin trainers frequently demonstrate this sense by placing rubber suction cups over a dolphin's eyes so it cannot see. Then the trainer tosses an object into the pool and asks the dolphin to locate it. Without hesitation, the animal dives and retrieves the object, to the applause of the appreciative crowd. In experiments, dolphins were able to find a three-inch ball almost 300 feet away. That's like a human spying a tennis ball from the opposite end of a football field.

A dolphin produces powerful clicking sounds that travel through the water, bounce off objects, and return to the dolphin. As many as 1,200 clicks a second are transmitted ahead of the dolphin like a beacon. They originate from the rounded "forehead" of the dolphin, called the *melon*.

As the dolphin swims, it moves its head from side to side to scan its surroundings. The echoes bounce back to the lower jawbone, which conducts the returning sound waves to the inner ear. Both the melon and the lower jaw are filled with an oily, jellylike substance, which amplifies sound waves. By the pitch of the returning echo and the time it takes to arrive, the dolphin can determine the location, shape, size, speed, texture, and density of the object. It can even learn about the interior of the object, almost like X-ray vision, except it is "vision by sound."

Both the forehead and the lower jaw play a part in echolocation.

There is evidence that dolphins use their sonar to see inside each other and into other animals. A trainer at Dolphin Reef in Israel found out how useful that skill can be. When the woman entered the dolphin pool, one of the dolphins circled her excitedly, aiming waves of sonar clicks at her abdomen. A week later the woman visited her doctor and learned she was pregnant.

At a "Swim with Dolphins" program in Florida, dolphins targeted their echolocation at a visitor's behind. When the man came out of the water, the dolphin trainer could not resist asking him if there was something unusual about his posterior to arouse such interest from the dolphins. "Oh, I still have some shrapnel from a war wound there," he replied.

*Dolphins' sonar clicks can sometimes reveal things about ourselves
we didn't even know.*

Sounds to Communicate

The clicks that dolphins produce to locate objects are often beyond our human hearing range. But dolphins produce a whole array of other sounds we can hear, including groans, barks, yaps, squeals, mews, and whistles.

Whistles allow dolphins to maintain contact within their *pod*, or group, or when meeting other pods of dolphins. Dolphins may whistle to warn of danger, to call for help, or to identify themselves, rather like humans introducing themselves by name. Scientists think the whistles may help dolphins hunt cooperatively or coordinate the movement of the group.

16

Human-Dolphin Communication

Louis Hermann is the director of the University of Hawaii's Marine Mammal Laboratory. He is a leader in the field of animal-language research. On any morning you might find him standing on a platform next to the dolphin pool playing "Simon says" with a bottlenose dolphin named Akeakamai (which means "lover of wisdom" in Hawaiian). When he waves, Ake waves; when he turns around in a circle, she turns in a circle; he gives her a hand signal to fetch a ball, and she responds immediately and correctly.

Hermann is not trying to develop a human/dolphin language, but he is trying to learn ways to communicate with them better and to understand how much they can learn. He studies dolphins' ability to understand and follow instructions in a made-up language, like a secret code you might make up between friends. He uses two approaches: sight and sound. With Ake, Hermann uses sign language. He strings together several hand signals to make a sentence, such as, "Person ball fetch," meaning take the ball to the person. With Phoenix, he communicates using different tones of electronic whistles.

Hermann is able to give the dolphins directions. They show that they can understand by following his instructions correctly. Can he get dolphins to communicate with each other using a made-up language? Hermann is now working on teaching two other dolphins an invented language they can use to communicate with each other. In doing so, he will try to understand the meaning of sounds they may make themselves as they perform the tasks he assigns them in their made-up language. In this way he hopes to analyze how dolphins communicate with one another naturally. In a way, it's like learning the word for "home run" in a foreign language by hearing batters use that word every time they hit a baseball out of the park.

Hermann is very careful not to attribute human meaning to dolphin behavior. He warns, "We should never expect animals to approach even the capabilities of the young child in language performance, as we would not expect a human to approach the capabilities of a dolphin swimming."

Mimicry

Dolphins are remarkable mimics, copying others' behaviors and sounds. Many of the "tricks" dolphins teach themselves are based on human behavior they've observed, such as when Kibby and Delphi move their mouths when they "speak." Another dolphin resident of the Dolphin Research Center loves to make the sound of a motorboat, which she

Captive dolphins often mimic their trainers' voices or sounds from their surroundings.

probably heard from a nearby marina. Others mimic the rhythm of their human companions' speech. Some can even reproduce the sound of a human laugh or the *brrrrr* of a Bronx cheer.

Some scientists have observed wild dolphins behaving like sharks. Ocean-going dolphins, like spotted and spinner dolphins, sometimes arch their backs and press their flippers downward. This is just what the gray reef shark does to warn others away from its territory. The researchers don't know if the dolphins' intent is to scare off sharks or to threaten other dolphins, but it is a convincing impersonation of a shark preparing to attack.

Intelligence

What is intelligence? Some people explain it as the ability to learn something, remember it, and apply it to another situation or in another way. The ability to use language is considered one sign of intelligence. So are curiosity, making up games, teasing others, and problem solving. Dolphins can do all of these to some degree.

At the Dolphin Research Center, a female that had just given birth was trying to protect her newborn from two aggressive male dolphins sharing her pool. The staff had tried unsuccessfully to move the female and calf to an adjoining pool without letting the males follow. Time after time, the female, slowed by her calf, could not swim fast enough through the open gate to escape the males that were in hot pursuit. Finally, the frustrated mother tossed her baby into the arms of a startled staff member and raced through the opening alone. The males followed eagerly. Then she dashed back into the first pen and a staff member slammed down the gate in time to separate the amorous males from the quick-witted mom and her baby.

Mother dolphins keep newborn babies close at their sides.

Chapter 4

Dolphin Family Life

Scientists are trying to learn more about dolphin social behavior, so that they can help return rescued stranded dolphins to dolphin society. Some dolphins prefer to go it alone, but most dolphins travel and feed in groups. A lone dolphin doesn't have as good a chance of survival as it does in a pod.

Mother and Child

Mothers and their babies make up the strongest social bond. After twelve months developing inside its mother's womb, a baby dolphin is born tailfirst, so that its blowhole comes out last. Sometimes another dolphin stands by to help push the newborn to the surface for its first breath of air. This "auntie" may support the baby until it is strong enough to surface on its own. Newborns are kind of floppy, and they aren't very good swimmers. It takes a few days for their flippers and fins to straighten out.

A newborn dolphin weighs an average of 25 to 40 pounds (compared to about seven pounds for a newborn human). It is three or four feet long, about a third as long as its mother. Its mother positions the baby at her side where it can ride on the "bow wave" she creates as she swims and where it is in the right spot for nursing. The mother contracts strong muscles that squirt milk into the baby's mouth like a water fountain. A newborn baby dolphin may nurse about every fifteen minutes day and night in fifteen-second bursts. The high fat content in the milk helps the baby grow rapidly and build up a thick blubber layer to keep it warm in the water.

For the first few days after its baby is born, a mother dolphin whistles to her calf almost constantly, helping it learn to recognize her by sound. A baby dolphin develops its own signature whistle, the unique sound that identifies each dolphin, and can mimic its mother's before it is a year old. Dolphin mother and child use their signature whistles to find each other when they are separated.

One researcher, Layla Sayigh, found that a baby male shapes its whistle to resemble his mother's, while a female calf creates a variation of her mother's whistle. Both males and females leave their mother's pod after several years, but a female offspring often returns when she has her first child. By having different signature whistles, mother and daughter avoid confusing the rest of the pod. Perhaps by learning to mimic his mother's whistle exactly, a male can always stay in touch with "home"

Mothers and their babies form bonds that may last a lifetime.

after he grows up, recognize brothers, and avoid courting his own mother.

Babies may nurse for up to two years, although they begin to capture and play with fish beginning around four to six months of age. The youngsters spend many hours a day in play, balancing objects such as stones, seaweed, and fish parts on their snouts and flippers, herding fish, pushing objects with their snouts, and learning other skills that will help them to hunt and avoid predators. Scientists believe that the many hours devoted to play are the way dolphins learn the skills they will need to survive as adults. It also helps them learn their place in dolphin society.

Family Ties

Young dolphins may stay with their mother's pod for several years, three to six years or even longer, before striking out on their own. When an offspring moves out, it is frequently to join another pod—a roving group of other youngsters ranging in age from three to thirteen. Just as you'd expect from a bunch of exuberant teenagers, a lot of energetic play goes on in these groups. They chase each other, nip at each other's fins, find and share objects, play catch with seaweed, and even blow bubbles. Two males often form long-lasting friendships. They may remain together for 10 to 15 years or longer.

Florida biologist Randall Wells has been watching bottlenose dolphins in the wild for many years. He has learned a great deal about the family structure and social behavior of several generations of dolphins. He has observed that male dolphins travel from one pod to another, staying for short periods and then moving on.

Family ties may remain strong even after offspring have "left the nest." Older children may return to visit or help out after younger broth-

In some places, helpful dolphins chase schools of fish into fishermen's nets.

ers or sisters are born. Researchers have observed older sisters and even brothers babysitting for younger siblings. This may be a way young dolphins learn how to be good parents.

Cooperative Hunting

Dolphins often gather in large groups to hunt together. One dolphin may go ahead to scout out feeding opportunities for them all. A pod of dolphins may surround a school of fish and herd them into a tight circle. Then the dolphins take turns charging into the school to feed. Sometimes dolphins chase a school of fish into shallow water or right up onto a beach, sliding up the muddy slope on their bellies.

Some scientists are investigating whether dolphins and killer whales produce loud sounds that stun their prey. In the Bahamas, dolphins were seen chasing fish right into the rocky coral reefs, so that the fish stunned themselves! Dolphins often slap fish with their tails, sending them flying out of the water, in a behavior scientists call *fish whacking*. The dolphins then swallow their stunned prey.

Dolphins sometimes congregate around fishing boats to feed on the fish or shrimp that escape the nets. Along the coast of Brazil, generations of fishermen have relied on dolphins to help them catch fish. Since 1847, at least three different generations of dolphins have driven the fish toward fishermen lined up along the shore. The fishermen do not train the dolphins, but rather take their direction from the dolphins, running up and down the beach to follow their lead!

Dolphins also congregate in groups for safety. Many adult dolphins show the scars of shark encounters. By pooling their senses, dolphins can watch out for predators, such as sharks and killer whales, from any direction.

*A Red Sea fisherman and a wild dolphin have formed an
extraordinary friendship.*

Chapter 5

How Dolphins
Help Humans

‿ᔆᕼᕚ‿

Dolphins and humans appear to have always had a special relationship, dating back to ancient Greek and Roman times. Two thousand years ago, a Roman scholar named Pliny the Younger wrote about a dolphin that befriended a boy in the harbor town of Hippo in North Africa. Each day the boy rode to school across the bay on the dolphin's back. Some legends claimed that sea captains in ancient Crete tethered dolphins to the bows of their ships to lead them through dangerous waters.

Abdallah offers Olin an octopus as a treat.

Many stories, spanning several centuries, have documented instances when dolphins rescued drowning sailors and pushed them to shore. (On the other hand, as dolphin trainer/researcher Karen Pryor once noted, "Of course, you don't hear from the drowning people whom the dolphins pushed *away* from shore.")

Best of Friends

In Egypt along the Red Sea, a modern-day dolphin/human friendship exists between a Bedouin fisherman and a female dolphin he named Olin. One day, Abdallah was casting nets into the Red Sea from his small fishing boat when a lone dolphin surfaced nearby. On an impulse, he dove into the water. The dolphin kept her distance, but she didn't flee.

The next day, she was back in the same spot. Each day she allowed Abdallah to come closer until finally she approached him to play. Now they are the best of friends.

Olin has brought prosperity to Abdallah's poor village of Nuweiba as tourists come from miles away to swim with the dolphin. Olin lets strangers play with her and pet her, but as soon as Abdallah enters the water she races to his side. Abdallah keeps a close watch on the visitors, who pay for the privilege of playing with Olin. He doesn't hesitate to step in if he thinks someone is harassing his finned friend.

Although Olin has been with Abdallah for over two years now, she hasn't deserted her own kind. She frequently goes off with other dolphins for short periods of time. Recently she gave birth to a baby dolphin, which Abdallah named Jimmy. Now that Olin needs more energy for nursing, Abdallah brings her fresh-caught fish to add to the food she

Most dolphin mothers are very protective of their newborns, but Olin allows Abdallah to join the family group.

hunts herself. Much to the amazement of dolphin researchers, Olin and her calf have stayed near Abdallah's beach. For the time being anyway, this dolphin family seems to be successfully bridging the worlds of finned and footed mammals.

Dolphin Therapy

In another part of the Red Sea, at Dolphin Reef in Eilat, Israel, is a 10,000-square-meter enclosure that is home to nine bottlenose dolphins. Early in the morning before Dolphin Reef opens to tourists, dolphin trainer Maria Steurer leads a timid little boy battling cancer into the pool. A friendly female dolphin named Domino swims up to greet him. He is overwhelmed at first by her 400-pound bulk, but once he strokes her smooth skin and hears the dolphin squeak with delight, he is won over. The sick boy has formed a close bond with Domino, returning to visit her after every surgery or chemotherapy session. "She gave him the motivation to pull through. Today he is in remission and seems to be doing well," Steurer recalls fondly.

This little boy is one of many sick or disabled children who have participated in Dolphin Reef's dolphin/child therapy program. Each swim lasts about a half hour, although a child may spend more time with the dolphins from the training platform, feeding them or giving them hand signals during a performance before an audience of awed visitors. "This gives the afflicted person a huge boost in self-confidence," Steurer explains. Some children help the trainers with everyday chores such as cutting fish or washing out buckets, which also helps them feel useful and capable.

The Dolphin Reef program was modeled on work done in the United States by David Nathanson at the Dolphin Research Center in Florida

ing from any number of illnesses, including heart disease, ulcers, or pneumonia. It could have been disoriented by parasites in its ears or brain. It could have been poisoned by a naturally occurring toxin in the sea—red tide. Or it could just be weakened by pollution—wastes from human activities routinely dumped into the sea. Whatever the cause, it will probably not live to see dolphin old age of 30 to 40 years.

Some causes of dolphin deaths are easier to trace. Many are caught by accident in tuna nets or drift nets. Some species of dolphins, particularly spotted dolphins and spinner dolphins, tend to travel with schools of yellowfin tuna. The dolphins swim at the surface while the tuna swim underneath them. Tuna fishermen may scoop up both tuna and dolphins in nets, drowning or injuring the dolphins. Dolphins are reluctant to jump over the nets, possibly because in doing so they would lose their most important sense, sonar, which only works underwater. Now, because of pressure from consumers to buy only "dolphin-safe" tuna (tuna caught by a method that does not harm dolphins), many fishermen use a procedure that pushes the back of the net underwater to allow the dolphins to escape.

Still, many dolphins and countless other animals are caught in drift nets spread across thousands of miles of ocean every night. Dolphins do not always cruise with their echolocation "on," so they may not detect the fine-mesh nets until it is too late. Other dolphins are killed on purpose for sport, or for food, or because they compete with local fishermen for food from the sea.

People who love dolphins can be part of the problem, too. Trading on the public's affinity for dolphins, boat tour operators in places like Florida, South Carolina, and Texas offer charter trips to take people to feed wild dolphins. Beach goers and anglers sometimes feed wild dolphins that come near shore. Once normally shy and timid, these dol-

Dolphins like this school of spotted dolphins are sometimes trapped in nets set to capture yellowfin tuna.

phins have grown accustomed to receiving handouts from humans. In some cases, dolphins have been fed hot dogs, candy bars, beer, and baited fish hooks.

As their feeding behavior changes from hunting to begging, some of these dolphins may no longer pass on important survival skills to their young. Scientists studied the offspring of six female wild dolphins routinely fed by tourists at a beach resort in western Australia. Only five of seventeen infant dolphins born to them survived. Some starved to death, perhaps because they weren't taught to hunt by their mothers. Others were struck by boats or attacked by sharks.

Protecting Dolphins

International treaties and laws are helping to change many of the fishing practices worldwide that harm dolphins and whales. In the United States, the Marine Mammal Protection Act and the Endangered Species Act have helped protect dolphins from harassment and killing since 1972. Laws like the Clean Water Act and individual actions to reduce pollution benefit dolphins, too, since dolphins are highly sensitive to poisons in their environment.

Marine Mammal Stranding Networks have been organized to help whales, dolphins, and seals that are hurt or beached. Rescuers have been able to rehabilitate and return many of these to the wild. Most coastal areas have teams of trained volunteers who respond to a report of a stranding. They can be reached through an aquarium, police department, or the regional office of the National Marine Fisheries Service, which enforces the Marine Mammal Protection Law.

Should dolphins be kept in captivity? That is a difficult question that greatly concerns animal rights activists, aquarium and zookeepers, and government agencies charged with protecting marine mammals. Keeping and displaying dolphins deprives them of their freedom and restricts their natural behavior to explore and to roam. On the other hand, there is nothing as motivating as seeing or touching an animal firsthand. It's like watching a game on television versus being on the field of action yourself. Still, does the emotional bond created by seeing a dolphin in person justify keeping animals for entertainment and education? Does it really lead to actively protecting others of that species that are threatened in the wild?

Many people are studying dolphins, both in captivity and in the wild, in order to learn how to conserve them. Their collective goal is to help dolphins survive and prosper by learning more about their health, their habits, and their habitats. Perhaps the most important thing that dolphins can teach us, in the end, is how best to safeguard all life in the sea.

Glossary

bends, the   A painful and potentially fatal condition due to changes in pressure as a diver ascends. Caused by gas bubbles bursting in the bloodstream. Also called "decompression sickness."

cetacean   Any whale, porpoise, or dolphin.

dolphin   A marine mammal with a pointed snout, streamlined body, and cone-shaped teeth.

dolphinese   The language that some scientists believed dolphins spoke to each other; no such complex language ability has been found in dolphins to date.

dolphin-safe tuna   Tuna that is caught by a method that does not harm dolphins.

drift net   A fishing net, often many miles long and set adrift on the open sea, that catches marine life indiscriminately.

echolocation   A series of rapid clicks; a method used to locate and identify an object by emitting a sound that is reflected back from that object.

fish whacking   The behavior in which a dolphin stuns a fish by slapping it with its tail.

follicle pits   Small indentations on a dolphin's snout that hold hair when a dolphin is first born.

hydrodynamics   The motion or action of water.

melon   A dolphin's rounded forehead, filled with a jellylike substance that focuses the dolphin's clicks at an object.

pod   A social grouping of dolphins.

porpoise   A marine mammal characterized by a rounded snout, a slightly round build, and spade-shaped teeth. There are six species of porpoises.

signature whistle   A dolphin's individualized whistle that identifies that animal to other dolphins; its "name."

sonar   Stands for **so**und **na**vigation **r**anging; a system using transmitted and reflected sound waves to detect the location of an object, used by submarines, bats, and dolphins; used interchangeably with echolocation.

temperate   A climate or ocean zone between cold and warm.

vocalizations   Various sounds dolphins use to communicate.